THE MYSTERY OF DIVINE POSSESSION

BY

OVIE BIAHI

Email address: oviebiahi@gmail.com
Phone: 08102993661

ISBN: 9798371629005

Acknowledgment

All Glory to God Almighty.

Contents

Introduction

(Genesis 23:1)

And Sarah was a hundred and seven and twenty years old: these were the years of her life, Sarah.

The right of every Christian is released under the unction of divine possession. Certain benefit comes with divine salvation. You are saved from bondage and pain.

It is free of charge the benefit that comes with every assignment in God. So long, as you do what is demanded of you by the spirit of God, all his blessings are yours to possess.

CHAPTER ONE

DIVINE HEALTH

(Genesis 23:1)

And Sarah was a hundred and seven and twenty years old: these were the years of her life, Sarah.

Divine health is simply the involvement of God in one's well being, both spiritually and physically. You can't be healthy without a balance on both sides. (3 John 1:2) Beloved, I wish above all things that thou mayest prosper and be in health, even as thy soul prospereth. It is both spiritual and physical health that creates a natural balance in your walk with God.

You can't say, you are healthy when you are mentally unstable and financially broke in God.

DIVINE PERFECTION

Divine perfection is the state of being spiritually and physically stable. God wants both for his people. The era of serving God and being broke is passed and gone: now is the era of kingdom wealth in God, no more spiritual blindness and financial foolishness.

DIVINE MATURITY

Divine growth in both realms is what creates harmony in one's soul. You can't serve God and end up weak on both sides, spiritually and physically. God wants the best of both realms for his people. Divine maturity helps you to attain both.

DIVINE EXPERIENCE

Life experiences are what make a man. All challenges and trials of life are to make you grow in grace and wisdom. Divine experience teaches you the true meaning of the world system and how it can be used to your advantage as a child of God.

CHAPTER TWO

DIVINE FULFILLMENT

(Genesis 23:2)

And Sarah died in Kirjatharba; the same is Hebron in the land of Canaan: and Abraham came to mourn for Sarah, and to weep for her.

Divine fulfillment is living a proven life that is acceptable before God. Nothing is more important than a life lived under divine will.

DIVINE FRIENDS

God wants what is best for you and the kind of friends that will be supportive of your vision.

DIVINE LEGACY

A journey well deserved and lived is part of God's plans for his people. God wants your name written on the sand of time.

DIVINE PURPOSE

Every purpose in God is given to aid and assist your life and not to destroy it.

DIVINE SPOUSE

God will never recommend a spouse that will destroy your career and ministry. God's choice is the best for you.

DIVINE RESPONSIBILITY

The assignment given to you by God is met and designed to sustain you till Christ comes. No assignment in God is too small to meet your needs and desire.

CHAPTER THREE

DIVINE CONFRONTATION

(Genesis 23:3)

And Abraham stood up from before his dead, and spake unto the sons of Heth, saying,

Life is designed for pleasure but with a cost. Every act of possession is accompanied by confrontation. Nothing given by God comes without a fight. Your fight determines your height in life. If you wish to go higher in life, then you should be ready to face the confrontation that comes with it, until your goals are met.

DIVINE DETERMINATION

Only the determined can obtain their possessions in God. You cannot possess your inheritance in God if you lack the guts to make up your mind to do so.

DIVINE MOTIVATION

Only a fool focuses on his disadvantages. You can make it in God if you believe in yourself enough to never give up the fight, till you obtain your possessions in God.

DIVINE ENCOURAGEMENT

Let the spirit of God guide you through your emotional limitations. Don't let your emotions get in the way of success. Draw encouragement from the spirit of God in you.

CHAPTER FOUR

DIVINE IDENTITY

(Genesis 23:4)

I am a stranger and a sojourner with you: give me a possession of a burying place with you, that I may bury my dead out of my sight.

When God is interested in a man, it shows. God's glory is released over his chosen to separate him from other people.

The glory of every assignment differs from others. Your natural identity is taken over by God's glory completely, that men could only see God's glory and not you anymore. Every glory comes with a task and a burden to carry out for God. God becomes you, while you no longer exist: your formal life is deleted completely from the scene.

DIVINE INTRODUCTION

Now this new glory of God on you changes everything about you. The life that you once knew is taken away and fresh life is introduced to you. You have to be taught all over for you to understand the new anointing of God on you.

Under this new anointing of God, no man can fake it because it reflects the glory of God. Your friends will change to accommodate your new friends in God.

DIVINE EXPLORATION

This new glory from God causes men to explore things about themselves that were unknown to them before now.

New powers, skills, talent, wisdom, and creativity are opened to you. You could do things that you completely couldn't do before. Your life and journey in destiny begin afresh to you and all men could see it also. But the day will come when all these things will be made clearer and understood by you.

DIVINE REQUEST

The anointing of transformation comes on those who ask the lord for a change of identity and glory. The anointing is released by God as he deems fit for you but you have to ask first.

DIVINE INTENTIONS

God has agenda and a plan for every anointing of his that is given to man. You have to be willing to pay the price of obedience to his instructions for his anointing to be released on your life.

CHAPTER FIVE

DIVINE RESPONSE

(Genesis 23:5)

And the children of Heth answered Abraham, saying unto him,

A divine response comes to align you with divine possession. You can only possess what has been given to you by God. God is the lifter of men and he does this through divine response.

DIVINE GENERATION

Every answer that comes from God is a life-changing experience. Your situation changes for the best and its effect continues from you to the generations to come.

God is a transgenerational God and he does this through divine response.

DIVINE REVELATION

God responds to your heart's desires through divine revelations. All you need is hidden in the word of God, the Holy Bible. If you can access its revelation then you can change your world.

CHAPTER SIX

DIVINE OBEDIENCE

(Genesis 23:6)

Hear us, my lord: thou art a mighty prince among us: in the choice of our sepulchers bury thy dead; none of us shall withhold from thee his sepulcher, but that thou mayest bury thy dead.

Divine obedience is paramount to divine possession. The essentiality of divine obedience can never be overemphasized if divine possession must be obtained. You can't possess the will of God without divine obedience.

DIVINE RESPECT

The act of obedience is a sign of divine respect and submission.

DIVINE IDENTITY

The glory and power of God only come on those who are obedient to the will and instructions of God. God cannot guide a man that is not after his will for his life.

DIVINE PRIVILEGE

Seeing life as a privilege helps you to appreciate the will of God over your life.

DIVINE PROVISION

Every benefit God has to offer comes on the platform of divine obedience.

CHAPTER SEVEN

DIVINE FOCUS

(Genesis 23:7)

And Abraham stood up, and bowed himself to the people of the land, even to the children of Heth.

Divine focus creates a concentration of attention on things that are relevant to the assignment of God committed to you. There is no better way to enjoy divine possession than divine focus. It helps you to stay concentrated on the task at hand.

DIVINE HUMILITY

Divine focus is triggered by divine humility. Total submission unto God's will helps you to stay concentrated on the things that are relevant to your assignment in life.

DIVINE RESPECT

Divine respect helps you to create an attitude of consideration or high regard for God. It causes you to remain dedicated to God's assignment in your life.

CHAPTER EIGHT

DIVINE WILL

(Genesis 23:8)

And he communed with them, saying, if it is your mind that I should bury my dead out of my sight; hear me, and entreat for me to Ephron the son of Zohar,

Life is designed under divine will and intentions. God created this world for his glory. Living under the will and desire of God is the only way to obtain divine possessions.

No man can please God outside his designee will and purpose for them. If divine possession is your desire, then get ready to obey the instructions of God to the letter.

DIVINE COMMUNICATION

God speaks and his will is unveiled to you when he speaks to you.

DIVINE CONDITION

Divine conditions are the rules and regulations guiding the will of God in your life.

DIVINE REVELATION

The will of God is revealed through the revelation of his written word.

DIVINE VOICE

The voice of God also communicates the will of God.

DIVINE DETAILS

The revelations of the will of God come in riddles and parables most time but through an intense inquiry from the spirit of God, it is made clearer.

CHAPTER NINE

DIVINE TRANSACTIONS

(Genesis 23:9)

That he may give me the cave of Machpelah, which he hath, which is at the end of his field; for as much money as it is worth he shall give it to me for a possession of a burying place amongst you.

Life is a business but done in God's way make it divine. A divine transaction is the understanding of the rules of engagement in God's kingdom. God's kingdom operates with different rules compared to this world. To take possession of your inheritance in God, you need an understanding of how kingdom blessing works.

DIVINE CONDITION

Life under God cannot be decided without his backing. No man under God has a mind of his own, all his choices are made under the guidance of God.

DIVINE CONTRIBUTION

There is a part of God that must be carried out by God while the rest is committed to you.

DIVINE VALUE

Learn to create value for the work committed to you by God. God may not tell you everything but wisdom demand that you handle all divine assignment with care and respect.

DIVINE LOCATION

Locations are strategic to divine allocation. Your location should be God's location. Let God decide and guide your step in every choice you make regarding where to dwell and reside in life.

CHAPTER TEN

DIVINE BALANCE

(Genesis 23:10)

And Ephron dwelt among the children of Heth: and Ephron the Hittite answered Abraham in the audience of the children of Heth, even of all that went in at the gate of his city, saying,

Divine balance is creating perfect harmony in your walk with God both physically and spiritually. There is a time for everything, a time to be spiritual and a time to be physical. You can't be both all the time but you can learn how to create perfect harmony within your soul by genuinely allowing the spirit of God to lead you both physically and spiritually.

DIVINE CREATIVITY

Your creative part as a human being come to light when there is a balance within your soul. You can't be creative when there is a conflict within your soul. Your soul needs perfect spiritual and physical harmony to be creative.

DIVINE BOLDNESS

Boldness is inspired when your soul is at peace within you both spiritually and physically.

DIVINE OPINION

It takes a divine balance to have a mind of your own. There are conflicting opinions and ideas out there but a divine balance helps you to harness them to your advantage.

CHAPTER ELEVEN

DIVINE FRUITFULNESS

(Genesis 23:11)

Nay, my lord, hear me: the field give I thee, and the cave that is therein, I give it thee; in the presence of the sons of my people give I it thee: bury thy dead.

Divine fruits are proof of God's involvement in your life. The blessing of God is released as fruits to God's people. It takes divine fruitfulness to lay hold on your possessions in God.

DIVINE OBEDIENCE

Nothing brings the blessings of God to his people like divine obedience. Obedience is the key to divine fruitfulness.

DIVINE INSTRUCTIONS

Yielding to divine instructions helps to bring God's fruitfulness in your life to manifestation.

DIVINE GIFTS

Understanding the gifts of God in your life helps you to be fruitful in your work with God.

DIVINE PROTECTION

It takes divine protection to be fruitful in life. To be able to sustain the blessing of God in your life, you need his protection.

DIVINE ABUNDANCE

It is the unlimited outburst of divine fruitfulness in one's life.

CHAPTER TWELVE

DIVINE HUMILITY

(Genesis 23:12)

And Abraham bowed down himself before the people of the land.

Choosing the will of God over yours despite the cost is what I call divine humility. Divine possession comes on the platform of divine humility.

DIVINE CONSIDERATION

Divine consideration is seeing the importance of God's instructions over yours.

DIVINE SUBMISSION

It takes submission to God despite your plan to be humble.

CHAPTER THIRTEEN

DIVINE REQUEST

(Genesis 23:13)

And he spake unto Ephron in the audience of the people of the land, saying, But if thou wilt gives it, I pray thee, hear me: I will give the money for the field; take it of me, and I will bury my dead there.

Learn to seek the help of other people in your quest to obtain divine possession. No man knows it all; you have to ask for the help of others people sometimes. Help comes from strange places when you least expect it.

DIVINE ATTENTION

Until you take a step of faith in life, the grace of God is limited. It is an act of faith that opens up divine possibilities and opportunities.

DIVINE SACRIFICE

The cost taken to obtain your goal in life is less compared to the reward that awaits you ahead. Do what is required of you by the leading of the spirit of God to obtain your goals in life.

CHAPTER FOURTEEN

DIVINE ANSWER

(Genesis 23:14)

And Ephron answered Abraham, saying unto him,

God hears prayer and he also provides his children with the right answer. God's ways may be different from a man but he sure knows when best to answer his people's prayers. Your possession will come at the right time in God.

DIVINE TIME

The timing of God may be different from ours but his time is always right.

DIVINE INSTRUCTIONS

The answers of God come as instructions and when obey turn into a blessing.

CHAPTER FIFTEEN

DIVINE DIRECTION

(Genesis 23:15)

My lord, hearken unto me: the land is worth four hundred shekels of silver; what is that betwixt me and thee? Bury therefore thy dead.

The leading of God is essential to obtaining divine possessions.

DIVINE VOICE

God speaks when his children require his guidance.

DIVINE REVELATION

The leading of the spirit of God comes through the revelations of his word to you.

DIVINE QUESTION

God cares about your affairs in life, so most time; he comes to ask for your opinions. He wants to know how you feel at that moment in time. What seeketh thou? What seeth thou?

CHAPTER SIXTEEN

DIVINE REVELATION

(Genesis 23:16)

And Abraham hearkened unto Ephron; and Abraham weighed to Ephron the silver, which he had named in the audience of the sons of Heth, four hundred shekels of silver, current money with the merchant.

Divine revelations are God's ways revealed to his people in plain English. You can only possess what has been revealed to you.

DIVINE ACCEPTANCE

You can't have access to divine truth and not get accepted by people. The more of God you are exposed to through divine revelation, the more of his glory your life reflects and men can't resist divine glory.

DIVINE UNDERSTANDING

Divine understanding is the knowledge of how divine revelation can be applied to your daily activities in life. It takes divine understanding to fully comprehend the reality of God's action in your life and to make meaningful use of divine revelations.

CHAPTER SEVENTEEN

DIVINE COMPLETION

(Genesis 23:17)

And the field of Ephron, which was in Machpelah, which was before Mamre, the field, and the cave which was therein, and all the trees that were in the field, that were in all the borders round about, were made sure

Nothing gives more satisfaction than the completion of the will of God in your life. It takes divine completion to obtain divine possession, where all God promises you to become manifested in your life.

DIVINE JOY

Arriving in destiny requires an unquenchable joy of the Holy Spirit. The devil's target is your source of joy and once he gets it, you will manifest his will without knowing. The spirit of God walks in joy and spread his joy in your soul and spirit man.

Never let the enemies take your joy from you; it is the way to arrive at divine completion satisfied with joy.

CHAPTER EIGHTEEN

DIVINE PRESENCE

(Genesis 23:18)

Unto Abraham for a possession in the presence of the children of Heth, before all that went in at the gate of his city.

Divine presence is the tangible glory of God in the life of his chosen. The presence of God carries the anointing of God in the life of his people. You need the presence of God to acquire your possessions in life.

DIVINE SPIRIT

Every child of God has the spirit of God dwelling within them as the Holy Spirit.

DIVINE ANOINTING

Divine anointing is the outpouring of the power of God on his chosen. The anointing of God separates the children of God from his chosen. The anointing is for a specific assignment and it is only given to those who have been called by God. Salvation grants you access to the presence of God while the anointing of God grants you access to the manifestation of God's power in a higher dimension.

CHAPTER NINETEEN

DIVINE TIME

(Genesis 23:19)

And after this, Abraham buried Sarah his wife in the cave of the field of Machpelah before Mamre: the same is Hebron in the land of Canaan.

Divine time is the inevitable progression into the future designed by God with the passing of present and past events. Divine time unveils the will and intentions of God as life progress for God's people.

Every possession you desire from God is tied to time and once it's time, their manifestation is inevitable and unstoppable.

DIVINE SEASONS

God created seasons in time to teach us the basic requirement needed to obtain our ultimate goals in destiny.

DIVINE PROTECTION

Every assignment in God has his protection on it. So long you stay under divine time as designed by God for your life; you are heavily protected by God.

DIVINE IDENTITY

A divine time comes with a different identity needed for the fulfillment of every task assigned to you by God. God's work requires a different phase of anointing. And every anointing comes with a new form of identity that suits your mission and purpose in God.

CHAPTER TWENTY

DIVINE LOCATION

(Genesis 23:20)

And the field, and the cave that is therein, were made sure unto Abraham for a possession of a burying place by the sons of Heth.

Divine locations are specific places designed by God for the fulfillment of every assignment from God. God never commits his task to a man's hand without a base for its accomplishment. Every work in God is in a specific location where its allocations and resource are available for possession.

DIVINE GROWTH

You grow in life when you are in your designed location by God. Growth becomes easy when you are in your place of calling or assignment.

DIVINE PROVISION

Your allocation from God is tied to a location and your place of assignment.

DIVINE PROTECTION

You are only protected by God when you stay in your place of assignment. Any assignment outside your location without God's approval is a call to certain doom.

Your protection is within your approval location by God.

www.ingramcontent.com/pod-product-compliance
Lightning Source LLC
La Vergne TN
LVHW041237150826
845673LV00008B/2402